The Scandal of Healthᵇᵉᵃʳ
Nurses, Waste (

Colin A. Baird ₐ

The Scandal of Healthcare: Nurses, Waste & Customer Service

By
Colin A. Baird and David L. Sundahl

Introduction

Twenty years of experience and research reveal two indispensable truths about hospitals and healthcare organizations that can no longer be ignored. First, those institutions neglecting the basic fundamentals of patient care, risk jeopardizing the quality and safety of care they provide. And second, nothing can have a greater short- and long-term impact on the cost of delivering healthcare services than nurses.

For more than 60 years the model of patient care has been changing. Hospital operations--the way work works--generally has fallen short in keeping pace with that change. Technology, protocols, and treatments are just a few of the dramatic shifts in recent years. But in the middle of all that change are nurses. In the middle of all the chaos of ringing bells and flashing lights are nurses. Underneath the hum and buzz of delivering healthcare to patients lie dysfunctional and costly processes, essentially forced onto nurses and their colleagues.

The concept of "Team Nursing" was designed and implemented during the early part of the 1950s. This new team-based model included staffing with a charge nurse, two or three Registered Nurses (RNs), along with a Licensed Practical Nurse (LPN) and a Certified Nurse Assistant (CNA) both of whom had less clinical training than an RN. This team was responsible for the care of eight to ten patients. Nursing stations were centralized, including connected supply rooms, linen stations, and equipment. Because patient rooms were arranged around the nursing station, it made sense to localize supplies and services. Likewise, connections to important people and information-- patient charts, doctors, pharmacists and phones--were centrally located too, just a few steps from the nurses station.

In the 1970s, a man named Gordon Friesen, an architect and logistics expert, proffered a simple notion: provide the highest quality of care possible for the individual patient at the lowest possible cost to the patient. Friesen's solution was built around the idea that the closer supporting people, equipment, and information were to nurses and their patients, the more efficient and effective nursing would become. The added efficiency would, as the thinking went, lead to better quality of care at continually less cost.

Friesen had landed on one of the few aspects of healthcare that everyone agrees on--patients are best served by having nurses with them in their rooms. Patients, their loved ones, executives, doctors, and nurses themselves all want to have nurses face-to-face with patients as much as possible. Yet, despite this common desire, due to myriad daily system failures, today's nurses are able to spend only a mere fraction of their time in direct contact with patients. Admissions and discharges take up most of this face-to-face time. Generally, patients see their nurses briefly every hour or two, which neither patients nor nurses find satisfactory.

Today the nursing station is all but gone. Medication frequency, dressing changes, and other prescribed care are ordered from a computer located in a patient's room, or just outside the door. In a scenario we have seen repeated hundreds of times, a nurse hurries to get medication, which is nowhere near the patient's room. As the nurse hustles to the med room, her aide asks for help with another patient, which delays the nurse's ability to deliver her original patient's meds. Now already several minutes

4

behind in getting medication, the nurse is assessing another patient who, say, needs supplies too. But unfortunately, those supplies are stocked in a different room from the medication. Leaving to get both, the nurse runs into a family member there to see their loved one. It just so happens to be her patient, and that patient needed their medication seven minutes ago. She provides a quick update and tells the family member they can see their loved one, and that she'll be right back. But then Transport calls. They're running late, which delays a patient's discharge, the one who's still waiting for the medication.

At present, nursing is a decentralized system of continually changing needs. As seen in the preceding paragraph, the failure to connect services to nurses increasingly burdens the daily activities of nursing. The difficulty arises for nurses because while nursing activities are *decentralized,* supporting services remained centralized. This mismatch in operational processes ensures each nurse will spend time hunting for, fetching, and clarifying what their patients need. This is further complicated by frequent failures in these mismatched processes. It's certainly true nurses need to be available for the patient. But when nurses aren't available, it's primarily due to hospital operations failing to meet the needs of nurses as the principal providers of care to patients.

Consider our proxy for hospitals across the country: AnyWhere in America Hospital (AWH). At AWH, medical equipment is upgraded regularly by contract with vendors in an effort to keep costs low, or to replace older outdated equipment. Usually this new equipment requires specific supporting supplies. A great example is an IV pump--a piece of equipment used all the time at AWH to introduce vital fluids and medications to the body. At AWH, leaders coordinate the new equipment supply needs for the upgraded IV pumps for each participating department during the roll-out phase.

However, many times implementation proceeds faster than expected. Confident in their planning and adaptability, AWH decides to roll the entire project out in record time, ahead of schedule. Unfortunately, Materials Management hasn't been notified of the timeline change and can only support the roll-out plan as originally designed. Nurses in various departments, lacking the proper supporting equipment and documentation, panic--adding tension to an already stressful job. Urgent calls begin as nurses from several departments, frustrated by the new equipment's impact, request large quantities of supplies that Materials doesn't have. The sudden flurry of ordering hits the Materials Supply Department, which then overcompensates by over-ordering, then overstocking. The overstocking causes both storage and delivery issues as problems begin to ripple outward.

The reality here is that healthcare organizations/hospitals (HCOs) function in a manner that requires nurses to focus more of their limited time and attention diagnosing systems needs than patient needs. Nurses scrambling for linen, supplies, equipment, or waiting to clarify a medication prescription are just a few examples. These types of process failures and hundreds more like them, happen thousands of times every day in every hospital across the United States. Sometimes these impacts affect the patient-- leaving nurses stuck caring for patients in a system that's failing them, or at least making it tremendously difficult to manage the operational chaos, rather than being able to maintain the health and recovery of their patients.

There is a serious scandal in healthcare: the toll that healthcare takes on the people who deliver it. The burdens of regulation, cost reductions, and quality initiatives piled onto nurses and other clinicians are undeniable. Without real operational gains and improvements, nurses will continue to be inundated with yet more of the same, and its impact will be evermore noticeable. When things go wrong operationally, it's the nurse who feels the pain first, leading to less-than-optimal care for their patients.

Chapter 1

Healthcare's Waste Challenge

The woes of healthcare and healthcare organizations (HCOs) are both big and small, well known and not. This chapter will outline some of the problems that HCOs and quasi-regulatory and regulatory bodies face as the US confronts the largest sector of its economy.

Cost constraints on healthcare organizations are enormous. Declining reimbursements, bundled payments of all flavors, a host of (often-unfunded) mandates, and a retiring Baby Boom generation continue to put a downward pressure on the profits of HCOs. When these demands are paired with the absolute necessity for higher quality outcomes, as well as new payment structures, HCOs find themselves scrambling to keep their organization and its services afloat.

Healthcare today faces a serious cost/quality conundrum. On the one hand, there is general agreement that healthcare is too expensive. Even though its growth has slowed, healthcare is still 22 percent of the US government's budget. On the other hand, the quality of healthcare delivered in the US is, frankly, middling. To resolve these competing demands, many organizations--both delivery and policy outfits--are constantly looking to confirm that high-quality outcomes for patients are cheaper than poor outcomes. Put another way, HCOs and others are looking to "make the business case for quality." This presumed business case is desirable for both profit and non-profit HCOs, and because of this, a great deal of effort and energy have been expended in the service of finding the link between cost and quality. At present, however, there are many partial cases, as in disease management for very sick patients. Still, there is no overarching, decisive evidence proving that high-quality work yields better margins-- except in the most trivial sense that payers are increasingly moving to some form of pay-for-performance.

The cost concerns of healthcare are not new. An article published in the January 3, 1904 *New York Times* outlined the financial woes of healthcare for New Yorkers. In that year, New York City alone was running a deficit of nearly $11M, approximately $300M in 2015 dollars. The article points out that the public budget simply would not be able to cover such a shortfall, which they noted was among the most pressing problems facing the city's finances. The unnamed author claimed that the needs of caring for people would inevitably lead the city into bankruptcy. The solution, he worried, was to continue to overburden nurses or to ration healthcare provided in hospitals, unless the city could raise enough money to create a sufficient endowment to keep pace with the growing cost and volume of healthcare in just New York City alone.

Challenging times continue to face healthcare today. Having greatly exceeded the rate of inflation, and with the added pressures of retiring Baby Boomers, Medicare spending will increase 35 percent by the end of this decade. In 2011, roughly 48 million Americans were receiving Medicare benefits as the first wave of Baby-Boomers retired. They have continued to retire at a record pace of nearly 10,000 per day. There will be more people receiving Medicare benefits in 2020 than at any time in US history. The Congressional Budget Office estimates that the aging population is responsible for 52 percent of Medicare's rapid increase.[1] By 2020 the cost of Medicare will consume nearly 30 percent of the total federal budget. And all of this is taking place in the face of uncertainty about the financial impacts attributed to the Affordable Care Act, including to what extent it will be implemented, and at what cost.

The infamous sequestration cuts that started in 2013 initially reduced Medicare spending by $10 billion. Even as cuts are sustained and expanded, Medicare's cost will continue to climb steadily. In 2013, the federal budget for Medicare was roughly $640 billion. In 2020, it will be $1 trillion!

Adding to this dismal picture, is the reduction in numbers of workers who support these programs. Worker-to-beneficiary ratios, the foundation for a functional Medicare system, will decrease more than 30 percent over the next ten years as more and more Baby-Boomers retire. With an increasingly aged population and a quickly shrinking tax base, Medicare's financial burden will be borne by fewer and fewer Americans, if it survives at all.

Despite this gloom-and-doom picture, in this book we assert that opportunities to reduce costs and recapture value are widely available. The waste-streams created by hospitals alone are themselves large enough that they have created entirely new and expanding markets. Growing numbers of businesses make tidy profits feeding off the *preventable* waste that hospitals and other HCOs generate. This waste-stream market is valued in the tens of billions of dollars each year, and is growing!

At our stand-in hospital, supplies and equipment at AWH are purchased daily. They are necessary to provide patient care and are second only to labor in terms of

---

[1] Background NO 2779 March 22, 2013

operational cost. Packages of these items arrive at the dock for Materials Management to receive. Deliveries to departments are made after procedures in Receiving have been completed. The person who ordered the product then puts the supplies away within the department, where nurses and other associates go to retrieve purchased supplies for their patients.

For any number of reasons, not all of the inventory is used. Since AWH represents the kind of hospital that can be found anywhere across the US, AWH accumulates outdated, unused, or just "no longer necessary" inventory and equipment, which are set aside. As it piles up, AWH looks for ways to get rid of the excess product. In good conscience, AWH can't just throw it away. After all, that seems wasteful.

So they call one of the growing number of vendors who specializes in assisting HCOs by purchasing their excess inventory or equipment. The vendor assesses the various items and then inspects them before making an offer. But the offer won't be close to what AWH actually paid. These vendors offer pennies on the dollar, and AWH graciously accepts the offer, since something is better than nothing.

These small purchasing organizations then pack up the inventory or equipment and send it to a holding area, where it will be cataloged, resterilized if need be, and then resold to smaller HCOs in the United States and abroad at near-retail prices. Worse still for the financial viability of an organization, some HCOs that don't know what to do with their excess inventory simply donate the surplus to local charities with very little, if any, documentation or accountability, which might have at least provided a tax benefit. Still, some just throw it away to be later taken to the landfill. Every HCO in America today

11

regularly follows one or more of these three courses in disposing of their excess inventory. These wasteful practices alone costs the US healthcare system nearly $15 billion annually. And it's preventable.

Another remarkable waste-stream often overlooked can be found in Nutritional Services. When patients are admitted at AWH, they're provided meals based on the hospital's dietary policies and the patient's care needs. Normally, patients at AWH order their own meals at the beginning of each day. These orders are assembled then brought to the kitchen and compiled together to determine all of the ingredients they'll need for the day. While the kitchen is busy cooking lunch, the hospital keeps humming along. But by lunchtime, roughly 20 patients have been discharged, transferred to another department, or transported to a different facility altogether. Often no one notifies Nutritional Services of these changes. Before any food leaves the kitchen, 20 meals have been needlessly wasted. In addition, some patients cannot eat what was ordered and others just don't have enough appetite to finish, so large portions of food are simply swiped into the garbage. At AWH, this happens so often that kitchen servers check with the patient first before delivering the tray, so they don't waste time unloading the tray carrier twice, once to serve it to the patient and once to throw it away. At AnyWhere in America Hospital, roughly half of the plates after every meal come back with food still on them.

In 2000, *Clinical Nutrition* published a study designed to understand the causes of continuing weight loss in hospitalized patients.[2] This seminal study was performed at

[2] High Food Wastage and Low Nutritional Intakes in Hospital Patients; A. D. Barton, C. L. Beigg, I. A.

a 1,200-bed university hospital and concluded that over 40 percent of hospital food was wasted. The study also discovered that greater than 10 percent of all trays brought back to the kitchen were left untouched, or not eaten, and then thrown away. These findings closely matched the data found by "The Worshipful Company of Cooks Centre for Culinary Research." In surveying more than 1,000 patient days, reported food waste ranged between 17 and 67 percent. In one facility, roughly 11 to 17 percent of all patient meals were completely missed altogether during a two week period.[3] The estimated cost of such waste for US hospitals, $100,000 for every 100 beds annually. Nationally, the United States wastes $1 billion each year by throwing food directly into trash cans!

These problems are not by design. Rather, the controls in hospitals have simply devolved to this point. Much of this is due to a failure to understand how systems function together within the larger framework of operations. More often than not, HCOs' divisions are treated like many individual parts. For instance, when reductions are required for financial reasons, most HCOs issue a directive for managers to cut, say, "10 percent across the board." This means that each department has to decrease its budget by 10 percent, even if the costs and consequences of cutting in one place create more serious repercussions elsewhere in the organization. Solutions to one single problem the organization encounters are often solved at the expense of many others.

Macdonald, S. P. Allison: (Clinical Nutrition 2000, 19(6): 445-449) Harcourt Publisher Ltd.

[3] High Food Wastage and Low Nutritional Intakes in Hospital Patients; A. D. Barton, C. L. Beigg, I. A. Macdonald, S. P. Allison: (Clinical Nutrition 2000, 19(6): 445-449) Harcourt Publisher Ltd.

Take medical supplies as an example. Many hospitals purchase automated supply systems as means of controlling supplies, their cost, and to provide nurses better customer service. However, decisions supply departments make are often driven by an isolated view of their own accountability. On the surface, this appears to be a logical next step in controlling costs, but it is destined to fail. Inevitably, the system's process requirements break down when someone with access predictably forgets to push a button. Stock-outs and overstock appear as compliance and service spiral downward, taking nurses' focus away from patient care and on to troubleshooting the many new failures these systems often create.

Back at our stand-in hospital, leadership at AnyWhere in America Hospital, has decided to lease an automated solution to solve their supply problems. Their supply expenses are over budget, and so too is labor. AWH needs to cut costs. The automated system is designed to eliminate stock-outs and, manual counting, along with reducing overall supply expenditures.

AWH is ready to implement the system. All of the supplies are set up correctly and all counts are dead-on accurate. The amount of inventory returned to Materials Management--the stock that didn't fit into the system--makes the project's success, at least on the surface appear promising. The system is in place and its "Go Live" occurs. Both the vendor and Materials Management are manning the supply areas to train nurses and whoever else has been authorized to access the system for supplies. Training takes most, if not all, of the first week to accomplish.

Beginning in the second week, stock-outs appear. They are few and far between at first, but then several per day begin popping up. The vendor is brought back in as a consultant to examine the problem. They quickly determine that staff aren't pushing the "Take" button when they take materials from the system.[4] To ensure they solve the problem, Materials Management at AWH is told to check and correct counts daily. This requires staff from Materials Management to physically go to the supply locations and count what is actually in the bin and make sure the system matches a process thought to have been eliminated with automation.

Another month goes by, and stock-outs persist. Only now stock-outs are a system-wide problem and AWH managers are meeting with the vendor, trying to create entirely new processes to mitigate the system's rigid operational requirements, none of which furthers the optimization of patient care, nor drive sound financial decisions.

At AWH, Central Medical Equipment (CME) begins each shift by rounding on assigned floors. CME staff have, among other responsibilities, the requirement to ensure that hospital nurses have sufficient type and quantity of pumps, beds, and equipment necessary in the service of patient care. Individual departments, such as a medical/surgical unit, need groups of pumps and other equipment stocked in clean supply rooms located on their units. The number of pumps per group are managed through a PAR level (periodic automatic review) established by management. This PAR

---

[4] While this may seem implausible to many, both of us have worked for organizations that ran into this very problem. Sundahl worked for a client who touted the cost savings of this system, saying that he had been able reduce materials handlers. As the system failed because "the nurses just won't press the $%*! button," this very smart executive had an a-ha moment. He solved the problem by *hiring people to monitor and manage the machines,* adding back more FTEs than he had cut the previous year by implementing the automated system. If an executive this smart could miss this irony, Sundahl figured anyone could.

level is supposed to last an entire eight-hour shift. CME staff will spend most of their shift cleaning pumps, along with myriad other duties.

Devices such as IV pumps and specialty equipment frequently require other medical supplies for their proper functioning. At AnyWhere in America Hospital, CME manages these supplies. CME staff take stock of supplies they'll need to fetch and replenish from their centralized storage area to various supply locations all across the hospital.

While this flurry of activity is going on, nurses from various floors are requesting specialty beds for patients beds that can only be ordered by CME. So while staff from CME are cleaning pumps and restocking supply locations, they're alerted by a pager system that requires them to stop working, find a phone, and check messages for bed requests. CME staff call the bed company to place the order. Then CME staff notify the nurse of the order and the estimated delivery time, only then returning back to the unfinished tasks at hand.

These constant and frequent interruptions to the work done by CME result in delays in patient care. And nurses, who continually deal with these constant costly system failures, unfortunately become really good at cleaning medical equipment and fetching supplies--something that is not (and should not be) a part of their clinical training.

The performance of nurses and their impact on quality is determined by many factors. In the end, though, all research on the quality of nursing care either concludes with the absolute necessity of support departments providing nurses with what they need, or assumes that these departments will do so. In other words, treating nurses as

customers, is at the heart of all work on the quality of care that patients receive.[5]

---

[5] For the purposes of this book we are utilizing the nurse (as customer) as they are the recipient of nearly every clinical and non-clinical services or request, which they then provide either directly or indirectly to a patient or physician.

Chapter 2

Nurses and "The Last Mile" to the Patient

Supply chains and other service industries, like telecom, worry about "the last mile"--the final step in delivering a product or service to customers. Like other industries, healthcare must connect most meaningfully to the patient, and the nurse is almost always part of (if not the sole manager of) that "last mile." The analogy of the last mile defines a deeply rooted issue about nursing's criticality (and that of other direct caregivers, like LPNs, CNAs, etc.). The "last mile" for hospitals in a new and rapidly changing environment may be the difference between keeping the hospital open or closing it down. And the cost of not addressing this "last mile" issue is perhaps the biggest threat--and opportunity--HCOs face.

One proposed method for closing that last mile of improving patient care while maintaining a reasonable workload for nurses has been to legally mandate nurse-to-patient ratios. There are growing numbers of legislative efforts, both state and federal, moving toward mandated ratios to ensure nurses aren't overloaded and patients are well cared for. To date, California is the only state with legislative authority to regulate nurse-to-patient ratios. But California is generally regarded as a bellwether of healthcare policy, so mandates are surely on their way across the US.

Certainly, nurse-to-patient ratios hold the potential to improve quality and reduce overburden. But such an approach, by itself, is flawed because it only reduces the number of patients the nurse has to work with without a concomitant reduction in the chaos that often characterizes their scandalous working environment.

18

The National Bureau of Economic Research in Cambridge, Massachusetts, published "The Effect of Hospital Nurse Staffing on Patient Health Outcomes," in which they concluded "that patient outcomes did not disproportionately improve with the introduction of nurse-to-patient ratios."[6] NBER's report did suggest that there may be "complementarities between nursing inputs and other (possibly unobserved) inputs and policies that lead to better patient care. Thus, improved nurse staffing might be crucial in improving patient care, but only in combination with other elements."[7] In other words, just changing nursing ratios alone will not achieve the desired benefits for the working environment of nurses or, most significantly, the quality of care that patients receive.

In the currently swirling whirlwind of overburdened nurses, about five percent of the nation's 2.7 million registered nurses have left the profession. Various estimates for future departures run at the 25 percent level. Some of this reduction will be due to retirement, but research indicates that nurse "burnout," as a percentage, is a serious risk to the future of healthcare. In a recent study of 40 hospital units, more than one third of nurses reported they intended to leave their position within the next year, citing "emotional exhaustion" and "lack of personal accomplishment," two key indicators of nurse burnout. And as "growing evidences has shown, nurse-burnout dramatically influences how satisfied patients are with their care."[8]

Job dissatisfaction among hospital nurses is four times greater than the average

---

[6] The Effect of Hospital Nurse Staffing on Patient Health Outcomes: Evidence from California's Minimum Staffing Regulation: Andrew Cook, Martin Gaynor, Melvin Stephens, Jr., and Lowell Taylor NBER Working Paper No. 16077 June 2010 JEL No. I10,I18,J08

[7] *Ibid.*

[8] Nurse Burnout and Patient Satisfaction: Doris C. Vahey, PhD, RN, Linda H. Aiken, PhD, Rn, douglas M. Sloane, PhD, Sean P.I Clarke, PhD, RN and Defino Vargas, PhD

for all other US. workers.[9] This is scandalous! Despite the fact that enrollment in nursing programs has increased by about 5 percent over the last few years, we are facing a future with fewer nurses than we need. In fact, there are approximately 126,000 nursing positions currently unfilled in hospitals across the United States.[10]

Even the American Hospital Association, a staunch national advocate for more than 5000 hospitals, measured satisfaction among healthcare employees and concluded: "that hospitals fail to meet the expectations of their employees far more frequently than employers in other industries do. Indeed, the data shows that health care employers are worse off than the national norm in every category."[10]

Finally, there is the growing number of nurses reaching retirement age. The average age of a working RN today is 55.3, and that age is increasing at a rate more than twice that of all other workforces in this country.[11] By 2020 the median age of a hospital RN will be 60 and there will be at least 400,000 fewer nurses available to provide care than will be needed.[12]

The scandal of healthcare is real and it is affecting patients, nurses, and many others. Organizations must, of course, be patient-focused, but we believe that the most

---

[9] Hospital Nurse Staffing and Patient Mortality, Nurse Burnout and Job Dissatisfaction; Linda J. Aiken PhD, RN, Sean P. Clarke PhD, RN, Douglass M. Sloane PhD, Julie Sochalski, PhD, RN, Jeffery H. Silber, MD, PhD

[10] From *Solving the Nursing Shortage*, "Listening to Nurses: Dissatisfaction and Burnout on the Job." http://www.afscme.org/news/publications/health-care/solving-the-nursing-shortage/listening-to-nurses-dissatisfaction-and-burnout-on-the-job

[11] Journal of the American Medical Association, June 14, 2000,283 (22): 2948-2954. as cited by Joint Commission on Accreditation of Healthcare Organizations

[12] 5 Buerhaus, Peter, Staiger, Douglas,Auerbach, David,"Implications of an aging RN workforce," Journal of the American Medical Association, June 14, 2000,283 (22): 2948-2954.

important proxy for patient-focused care is excellent internal customer service for nurses, since they are involved in nearly every aspect of direct patient care.

Because nurses are essential to better and cheaper healthcare,[13] [14] and because their work life is burning them out and seems destined to become more complicated as fewer of them care for more patients, we contend that organizations must and can succeed by looking at nurses as "customers" of internal services. By taking a system view of meeting patients' needs, HCOs can work to ensure that their nurses always have exactly the information, equipment and supplies their patients need at exactly the right moment.

---

[13] Aiken LH, Clarke SP, Sloane Dm, Sochalski J, Silber J. Hospital nurse staffing and patient mortality, nurse burnout, and job dissatisfaction. JAMA 2002 Cot 23;288(16); 1987-93
[14] Anderson S. Deadly consequences: the hidden impacts of America's nursing shortage(monograph on the internet). Arlington, VA: National Foundation for American Policy; 2007 Sep {cited 2008 Apr 21}

Bethany, a nurse who has worked at AnyWhere in American Hospital for just over a year, swipes her badge at the time-clock near the female locker room before heading in. Once inside, she heads to her locker, where she'll hang up her stuff, grab a stethoscope, and then it's off to shift report. There nurses discuss patients' needs, current conditions, or other tasks needing to be performed while caring for patients at AWH. Tonight, Bethany has one patient being discharged, an inbound admission, two surgical patients, and one patient who is now mostly self-care.

Bethany looks through notes prioritizing her patients as she heads down the hall to see the first one of the evening. She stops at the door, politely knocking.

"Hello," Bethany calls to the patient, Tanya, as she enters. "My name is Bethany, and I will be your nurse this evening." As she gets closer to Tanya, she asks, "How are you feeling?"

Tanya, exhausted from surgery, answers groggily, "I'm still in a bit of pain."

"Well, then," Bethany replies. "let's get your pain under control." She makes her way around the other side of the bed to the computer, where she'll access Tanya's medical information. "According to your chart, it looks like you can have more pain medication. But first, I need to document your vitals, okay?" Bethany smiles.

Tanya agrees and Bethany quickly assesses her, then it's back to the computer to update her information. Bethany informs Tanya that she'll need to go and retrieve her pain medication, and she will be back in flash. Then it's out the door and down the hall to grab the medication.

On the way, her phone rings. "Hello, this is Bethany, Med-Surge One. How can I help you?"

"Hi, Bethany, this is Jim from Patient Transport. I'm returning a call about a patient's discharge. It was requested a while ago."

Bethany quickly cuts him off.

"Jim, yes, hi. I have a patient who will be discharged at four p.m. this afternoon. I'd like to arrange a wheelchair for transportation."

"Sure. Can do." Jim says. "We'll have staff there with a wheelchair at four."

Bethany thanks Jim, hangs up the phone, and again heads down the hallway to get Tanya's medication. Along the way, Bethany begins to wonder if that particular patient is really ready to be discharged. To be sure, she stops at the secretary's desk on her way to the med-room. "Are the discharge instructions printed and ready to go for the patient in Room 300?"

The unit secretary looks up, then back to her computer with a few clicks of the mouse, then says. "They're ready."

"Okay, thanks." Bethany replies. "I'll be back to get them."

The secretary begins quickly gathering information about the patient and whether or not they are truly ready to be discharged. "Hey, Chris!" she shouts softly. "Check on the patient in Room 300 and see if they are ready to be discharged."

Chris, a nurse's aide who works in that department, looks at the secretary, puzzled for a moment, then points his finger toward the room. The secretary nods back, saying. "Yes, that one!" and then motions Chris to go in and check on the patient.

Just down the hall and around the corner, Bethany finally logs onto AWH's medication dispensing system so she can retrieve the needed medication for Tanya. "Sometimes I wish I didn't have to scroll through all these profiles looking for my patient's name," she mumbles under her breath. Finally finding the right one after looking through forty or fifty of them, Bethany selects the appropriate medication and the med-control drawer pops open. She takes the medication, closes the med drawer, logs out, and heads back down the hall toward the secretary's desk to find out if everything is ready for the patient in Room 300.

Stopping at the secretary's desk. Bethany asks, "Is all of the paperwork ready?"

"The paperwork is ready," the secretary explains, "but the patient still needs their IV taken out."

Bethany looks down at her watch. It's 3:45 p.m. "Okay," Bethany says, "I will be back in a flash. I need to get this medication to a patient first."

Quickly she heads back to see Tanya, who is still waiting for medication.

Just before she reaches her room Bethany's phone rings.

"Hi Bethany. This is Jim from Patient Transport again. We're going to be a bit late, maybe ten minutes or so."

"Okay, well, let me know if you're going to be later," she requests.

Bethany looks at her watch. Its 3:50 p.m. I have *twenty minutes*, she says to herself as she's walks into Tanya's room.

"I'm back with your pain medication," Bethany tells her as she begins to hunt around the patient's room looking for cups. Bethany cannot find any cups and is now very frustrated, telling Tanya who is in pain and has already been waiting that she'll

24

have to wait just a little bit longer as she has to leave and retrieve one more thing.

Bethany quickly walks back to the supply room, some thirty feet away, to get a cup. However, she can't find any cups in the supply room, either. Storming out of the supply room, she bumps into Chris, almost knocking him over. "Oops, sorry, Chris." Bethany quickly apologizes. "Hey, I need paper cups, do we have any?"

Chris, Bethany's aide for the evening, tells her, "We had some on the other side of the secretary's desk. But I think we may be out." Bethany spots them and now is busy walking around the other side of the secretary's desk, grabbing the last remaining cups from the counter, then carrying them back to Tanya's room with her.

Quickly she stacks the cups on the bathroom sink for later minus the one she fills with water, and hands both the cup and the medication to the patient, motioning to Tanya to take the medications. "If you can't drink all the water, that's okay," Bethany says as she is entering information into the computer. "I'll be back to check on you to see how you're feeling."

Tanya replies, "Okay," as Bethany walks out the door.

She stops and looks at her watch. It's 4:05 p.m. *I've got to get my patient ready for discharge*, she thinks, making her way back down the hall to the secretary's desk, grabbing the patient discharge packet along the way as she heads into Room 300.

"Hello, I'm Bethany and you're being discharged today, correct?" Bethany says with a big smile.

"Yup, I've been here long enough," Mike says.

She informs him that it's time to take his IV out. Bethany further explains that,

25

once that's been completed, they'll review Mike's discharge instructions, and then he's free to go. Bethany heads to the cabinet where the needed supplies are to remove the IV, only to find it is missing her size glove--an item required to do the job. Her head drops. Bethany says, "I'll be right back. I have to get a few things," as she heads out the door.

Once outside Mike's room, she again heads down the hall toward the supply room when suddenly, her phone rings. She answers while continuing her way to the supply room.

"Hi Bethany, this is Jude in the Emergency Department. I can see in our system that you're ready for a patient to be admitted. Is that correct?"

"Yes, we're ready on our end."

"Can we admit them now?" Jude asks.

"You sure can, I'll be waiting." Bethany hangs up and looks at her watch. It's now 4:10 p.m. *Patient Transport should be here already*, she thinks as she arrives at the supply room. Quickly, she walks in to get her size glove, but to her surprise, it is empty too. Bethany darts out of the supply room on a mission to find a computer so she can order the supplies she'll need to care for Mike, still waiting to be discharged. And now delayed, she'll need to order it "stat," because Patient Transport is on their way and will be waiting for her. She grabs her phone and dials Materials Management.

A phone clerk answers, and Bethany quickly gets to the point. "Hi, my name is Bethany from Med-Surg One. I just sent a stat order for supplies. Could you tube them to me as quickly as you can?"

26

"As soon as your order comes through, we'll process and send it up straightaway," the clerk replies.

"Thank you." Bethany hangs up. She looks at her watch it's 4:15 p.m. and Transport still hasn't arrived. She heads back to the secretary's' desk to inform her of the order and ask that she be on the lookout. "Please call me when they arrive," Bethany asks, then walks off to see yet another patient.

"Good afternoon," Bethany says to Kate as she walks in. "How are you feeling today?"

Kate responds by telling her that she doesn't feel well and informs Bethany that the doctor just left, suggesting more IV fluid be given. Bethany logs on to the computer in the room.

"You're right," Bethany assures Kate. "I will be right back with your IV, but before I go, I'll need to check your vitals. Would that be okay?" Kate nods in agreement. Bethany makes her way to the bed, assesses her vitals, then records them by entering the data electronically into her electronic health record. "I will be right back to get you set up." Bethany leaves the room to retrieve what's needed.

As Bethany is getting ready to walk out of Kate's room, the phone rings. "Hello," Bethany says as she steps out into the hallway.

"Yeah, hi, Jim again. We are running late and wanted to let you know."

Bethany is by now a bit upset about another delay. Stressing, she asks. "What time do you think you will actually be here?"

"About four thirty," Jim replies.

27

Unexpectedly, Bethany's phone beeps, "Hold on, Jim, I have a call on the other line." Bethany quickly switches lines.

"Hi Bethany, your supplies have arrived and they are on my desk waiting for you," the secretary explains.

"Okay. On my way," she replies. Placing the phone back in her pocket as she hustles toward the secretary's desk. Suddenly, she realizes Jim is still waiting on the other line. She stops, grabbing the phone from her pocket.

"Sorry about the lag time, Jim. I almost hung up on you."

"No problem, Bethany" Jim tells her. "We'll have someone there around four thirty."

Bethany agrees and hangs up. Finally she makes her way to the secretary's desk. She can see the supplies sitting on the counter, grabbing them she heads into Mike's room.

"I'm back" she tells him, "Now, let's take that IV out, shall we?"

"I'm ready," Mike tells Bethany.

Moments later she says, "There you go, all set. Now here are your discharge instructions. If you have any questions, let me know. Make sure you take all your medications as prescribed. Transportation Services will be here at four-thirty to pick you up." She looks at her watch, and it is 4:30 p.m. "Okay, let me know if you need anything, and good luck," Bethany says with a smile as she walks out of Mike's room.

She still needs an IV pump for Kate, so Bethany heads for the equipment room. Reaching it, Bethany walks in, only to find no clean IV pumps. Now it's out the door, down the hall, around the corner past the supply room and into the dirty room to retrieve and clean an IV pump. She grabs a gown, a mask, and gloves from a rolling cabinet just outside the door. Now in protective gear, she heads in to clean an IV pump she needs for Kate. After ten minutes or so, she's finished cleaning the pump and can now take it with her. She takes off her protective gear, throwing them into a garbage can. Grabbing her clean IV pump, she heads back toward Kate's room.

Bethany stops at the supply room first, where she needs to pick up several different supplies before making it back to Kate's room. Leaving the pump outside the door, she enters. Bethany quickly finds the IV supplies and tubing, but she cannot find the IV fluids Kate needs. In disbelief, she roots around the supply cabinet, only to discover they're stocked-out. Her phone rings.

"Yes, this is Bethany," she says exacerbated.

"Bethany, this is Chris. I think we have a problem. Could you come to Room 312?"

"I'll be right there," she tells Chris as she leaves the supply room, grabbing the IV pump and taking it with her along the way.

Walking in, she sees Chris picking up dirty linen. "I can see the problem already," Bethany says to Chris, who's busy rolling up dirty linen from off the bed.

Chris asks "What time is the patient coming?"

"I don't know. They called at four-ten to verify and said they would arrange the admit," Bethany replies. "I just assumed they would send the patient when they were ready. But if they're having the same amount of trouble with Transportation Services as

29

I am, who knows."

Bethany searches the room for fresh linen to help Chris make the bed. There is a light tap on the door, and a voice shouts, "Hello!" into the room. Bethany looks up at Chris and they both look toward the door. A man walks in, pushing a patient in a wheelchair.

"Hi, I am from Patient Transport. I have your admission from the Emergency Department. And they also told me that I am supposed to pick up another patient who's being discharged." he says.

Bethany looks at her watch it's 5:00 p.m.

"You were supposed to be here a half hour ago," She says, shaking her head, trying her best not to get flustered by the predicament they're in. "It may take a bit to work this out," she tells the man. Frustrated, Bethany grabs her phone and calls the secretary again. "Room 312 needs to be cleaned right now!" Bethany explains. "We actually have a patient sitting in a wheelchair, waiting for a bed."

Embarrassed, Bethany leaves the room, informing Chris on her way out the door that he will need to fetch linen to make the bed, and that she'll be right back. She still needs to order IV fluids for Kate, who is still waiting to be cared for, along with several other patients who have not seen Bethany yet today.

Chapter 3

Nurses as Customers Under New Management

The shocking cost and magnitude of waste that hospitals and HCOs generate is only part of the scandal of healthcare. It is a symptom indicative of a larger, yet more costly problem: the exasperating conditions in which nurses and other caregivers must work. For non-nurses, the story of Bethany might seem overly dramatic; for nurses, the story is dishearteningly familiar--probably not even qualifying as a truly tough hour of work. Nurses like Bethany experience an increasing sense of frustration and exhaustion, and in many cases leave the organization, worn out by the task of swimming upstream against an incessant tide of small, annoying problems.[15]

There is a clear and distinct difference between what leaders perceive as current nursing functions and what they actually are. As the nurse executive and researcher, Sharon Pappas, has said, "Nursing is more than a component of the hospitals infrastructure. It is an intervention, one that is instrumental in achieving operating efficiency and the success of the healthcare organization."[16]

Shared expectations are social norms that govern most aspects of human interactions that implicitly, and sometimes explicitly, define a specific set(s) of expectations, given the type and context of interaction. Suppose you were a college

[15] Why Hospitals Don't Learn from Failures: ORGANIZATIONAL AND PSYCHOLOGICAL DYNAMICS THAT INHIBIT SYSTEM CHANGE Anita L. Tucker & Amy C. Edmondson: CALIFORNIA MANAGEMENT REVIEW VOl. 4S, NO 7 WINTER 2001

[16] JONA Volume 38, Number 5, pp 230-236 Copyright B 2008 Wolters Kluwer Health | Lippincott Williams & Wilkins THE JOURNAL OF NURSING ADMINISTRATION The Cost of Nurse-Sensitive Adverse Events Sharon Holcombe Pappas, PhD, RN, CNAA, BC

student sitting in class. You'd expect the professor to show up on time and teach the class. But what if she came into the classroom late, crawling on her knees, dragging her bag behind her as she entered the classroom? Surely this isn't something you'd expect, and is an extreme example. Nonetheless, it illustrates a valuable point: the need and value of stable shared expectations.

With nursing, often expectations change. Remember, nursing is a system of continually changing needs. When patients' needs change, so too do the needs and requests from the nurse. Jody Hoffer Gittell, a professor at Brandeis University's Heller School who studies frontline workers' impact on customer service, expresses best the importance of shared expectations in customer service: "Customer service is directly influenced by the shared expectations participants place on the work process itself, what participants expect to happen, and those relationships in turn are influenced by the nature of their communications, how well participants define, share and develop knowledge and implement solutions."[17]

HCOs all too often have characterized customer service solely by the interactions between the nurse and/or other direct caregivers and the patient. However, there is another relationship here, and it has been proven as a fundamental ingredient to customer service--one that positively affects nursing engagement and moves patient satisfaction scores northward while dramatically reducing operational costs--*the relationships that exist between hospital support services engaged in providing a*

---

[17] Relationships between Service Providers and Their Impact on Customers, Jody Hoffer Gittell, Journal of Service Research 2002 4: 299

product and/or service to a customer, in this case a nurse.[18] [19]

Outstanding customer service is a mutually reinforcing "process of interactions" between both support services and nursing.[20] Each participant is important, their responsibility for sharing their knowledge of the work process is vital, and their shared knowledge is integral to customer service. In the context of any work process, "shared knowledge" is actually a *characteristic* of the work. "And it is the foundation in which learning occurs, but most importantly, shared knowledge leads to knowledge thats implicit."[21] Therefore, creating an understanding and expectations that are relevant and reliable are required and critical to improved quality and lower costs for healthcare delivery.[22]

As a customer, the nurse has numerous "suppliers": Materials, Dietary Services, Transportation Services, Respiratory Therapy, etc.[23] Many aspects of this customer-supplier relationship contribute to the care of patients in important ways. Suppliers need to coordinate their delivery of supplies and services to patients/nurses. We have seen all too often that Respiratory Therapy arrives just after Transportation Services has taken a patient to Radiology. In a clinic setting, we have seen something similar: the

---

[18] *Ibid.*

[19] Although we mostly use hospital settings, there are many environments that constitute an HCO. For instance, in a clinic, it may make sense to think of the physician, medical assistants, PAs or someone else as the central "customer" of other services for patients.

[20] Relationships between Service Providers and Their Impact on Customers, Jody Hoffer Gittell, Journal of Service Research 2002 4: 299

[21] Decoding the DNA of the Toyota Production System by Steven Spear and H. Kent Bowen, HARVARD BUSINESS REVIEW September-October 1999

[22] Relationships between Service Providers and Their Impact on Customers, Jody Hoffer Gittell, Journal of Service Research 2002 4: 299

[23] We borrow here the terminology and guidelines for designing work systems used by Steven Spear and Kent Bowen from their article, "Decoding the DNA of the Toyota Production System."

orthopedic PA arrives to assess a patient while they are getting an x-ray. Suppliers of services to patients and the people who care directly for them should coordinate both when they deliver services to a patient, and in which order. For instance, it makes no sense for an orthopedic surgeon to see a patient in the clinic before an x-ray is available, when it's known in advance that the patient will need one. This coordination is essential.

Nonetheless, these various services cannot coordinate without direction from the nurse. Yet a nurse is often too busy to accommodate each service. However, a nurse or a standard routine can identify which supplies and services are required and in what order. Nurses, PT, Radiology, physicians, and others should--as work is made clear-- never show up to a room where multiple services are there at the same time, nor should they ever have to hunt for a patient.[24]

In addition, suppliers will always know more about what they provide than customers do. We regularly observe nurses calling down to Materials Management, only to have the wrong item ordered. Both the nurse and the materials handler complain about this. Nurses blame Materials Management, Materials Management blames nurses. Usually, Materials Management demands clarity, say, in the form of a vendor SKU, from resistant nurses. Nurses resist this for good reason: the ins and outs of inventory and supplies is not their area of expertise--nor should it be.

Assessments, planning, and coordination with other services in (and out) of the

---

[24] The details of how to design a reliable system such as this will be covered in more detail in subsequent chapters.

hospital yield an overwhelming amount of data. And it gets worse every year. Nurses interact with an average of five to seven departments, in addition to the same number of patients, during any given shift. And she'll make hundreds of process connections each day. In addition, a growing body of evidence shows we humans have a limited amount of decision-making power per day.[25] As the number of decisions nurses must make in a given day increases, the lower quality those decisions become. If we continue to allow the job of nursing to be so burdensome, we waste more of their limited and essential brain power deciphering events or failures that take away from good clinical decision-making.

Another problem we've observed is that in an effort to change cultural norms, managers constantly find themselves in a position where their staff lob problems "over the wall" to them. Since most managers in HCOs often spend much more time in meetings than they do on their units or departments, they leave staff to deal with the constant barrage of process failures, on their own.

A CNO once captured this problem with brilliantly acute insight as her facility was going through a large-scale renovation. She excitedly told one of her high-performing nurse managers that the facility plan placed the manager's office in a glass-walled space directly adjacent to the nurses' station. Her manager said, "But how will I get my work done?" The CNO was, to say the least, disappointed by this question. It would be easy to blame this nurse manager for her conception of what her work really is. But

---

[25] See Speier C, Valacich J, Vessey I. "The Influence of Task Interruption on Individual Decision Making: An Information Overload Perspective." Decision Sciences. 1999; 30(2):337–60.

organizational norms and prospects for advancement naturally draw managers out of their units; no one was ever promoted for opting out of meetings. Senior leaders who consistently worry about organizational culture can begin to change this through granting permission, even giving encouragement and praise, to managers who opt out of meetings to serve their staff in removing the friction in current work systems, leading to smooth operations that ensure exceptional quality at the lowest possible cost.

Leaders and managers must also see themselves primarily as teachers, guides that teach their people to identify issues in a positive way and to participate actively in improvement efforts with their employees. Staff must keep the wheels turning, but they must work hand-in-hand with their managers to design effective countermeasures leading to durable improvement. We have found that when approached this way, nurses and other healthcare employees are willing to try new things for the benefit of the organization. When managers interact with staff as coaches and as the first line of defense in solving system problems, nurses become powerful allies in lowering cost and improving quality--the holy grail of managerial work.

When leaders enable managers to be on the unit, they must then reverse the normal allocations given to understanding and solving problems.[26] In most organizations, leaders raise an issue that needs resolving, brainstorm solution ideas, and then implement the best candidate. What naturally follows from this is a great deal of work to get "buy in"--really compliance. And there's the rub. Getting people to act on a proposed solution is much more difficult than it seems it should be. In fact, when

---

[26] Details on the method for doing this are below in Chapter 5.

seeing solutions to problems utilized in the organizations we have worked with, often the first question of frustrated managers is, "How do you manage to get staff and doctors to get buy in?" The answer, is that consensus on a fix, for a problem, is easier if managers spend most of their time gaining consensus on the problem and its causes.

This new framing of managerial work inverts managerial practices traditionally seen as effective. Solutions neither come from taking suggestions from staff, nor from designing systems in meetings. Rather, successful sustainable solutions begin with managers doing "legwork," the observations required to understand a problem and its causes. As managers do this, they also "shop" their understanding of the issue they seek to resolve. Buy in, a willingness to work differently, even when it requires staff to make extra effort, turns out to be the natural byproduct of a leader gaining agreement on a problem and its causes. In fact, we have found that solutions to problems and agreement by staff to implement these solutions become almost trivial when people have a shared view of a problem and its causes.

There are three important rules of thumb we have found that make managerial success easier. The first is that 80 percent of a manager's effort should be devoted to understanding an issue. Implementation through some iterative testing should only occupy about 20 percent of the effort. The second is that, following the scientific method--which we address in detail in Chapter 5--managers should isolate single aspects of problems to work on. That is, they should sequentially work each facet of a problem. This allows a manager to perform single-factor experiments. If we take the scientific method seriously as the working method for improving operation, we must make it clear which causes lead to which effects. The typical multi-faceted or whole-problem approach to resolving issues literally makes it impossible to know which countermeasures yielded success and which ones didn't. Lastly, we have found that if a manager guides her team through the scientific method but discovers they haven't solved the problem and says, "We got this wrong. I'm going back to get a better understanding of what's happening," morale soars.

As nurses become willing to seek help in solving problems--whether they are contributing to the problem or not--leadership has changed the elusive "culture." The concept of "nurses seeking help" seems counterintuitive to the daily operations of patient care. But, we have found nurses to be the most reliable identifiers of problems for patients, as well as our greatest ally in improvement efforts that significantly reduce the cost of delivering care to patients.

These recommendations sound simple. But simple ain't easy. Frontline managers are under constant pressure to move faster, solve more issues, save more money--and now! But we have found that the sequential approach to problem solving using the scientific method, is *much* faster than the traditional method. Without fail, when we set the expectation of single-factor experiments, leaders say, "What you say sounds great, but we've got to do this faster! This problem-solving process simply takes too long." But this shows a misunderstanding of how long it currently takes to achieve sustained resolution of important problems.

Consider medication reconciliation, the persistent bugaboo of patient safety. We have found that virtually every manager in every HCO has worked hard and with great intelligence and diligence on this issue, and yet serious problems persist. It may seem that by decomposing the various aspects of the problem, studying them through observation, and gaining agreement on each sub-problem and its causes takes too long. But, without putting too fine a point on it, how could it possibly take any longer than our current efforts to resolve this chronic problem--or any other for that matter? Serious issues such as med reconciliation, medical errors, supply stockouts, missing equipment, insurance changeovers, and many, many more predate the working life of *every* leader! Consequently, we propose that the sequential, single-factor approach--the scientific method--be incorporated into the managerial work practice. But in order to start that train down the tracks, leaders must learn about their organization and then choose a focus for the organization.

Chapter 4

Learning through Observing and Creating Focus

A great deal of variability and adaptation has to happen in a healthcare setting. This, above all, is why HCOs should use the many, small-problem approach to shaping an organization that enables nurses to get what they need, when they need it to take care of patients. This approach also helps managers and staff to pin down many of the uncertainties common to healthcare. We are not suggesting that HCOs try to predict or control what can't be predicted or controlled; quite the contrary. To be successful, hospitals and HCOs must rely on the adaptability and experience of, above all, nurses.

A colleague of ours, Anita Tucker, once drove home the superiority of building habits and capabilities using the so-called "incrementalist" approach to scientific improvement over the large "vertical" project approach. Using data on sentinel events for a 14-year period, she discovered that the 80/20 rule simply doesn't work. In order to resolve 80 percent of the problems leading to sentinel events, she found, an organization would need to resolve fully 59 percent of the 21 problem types, such as medication error, infections, and wrong-site surgery. This means that an organization would need to undertake 13 major initiatives to resolve 80 percent of the problems leading to disaster. To make matters worse, the third largest problem type is "other, less common causes." That is, one of the biggest projects an organization would need to undertake would be resolving one-off problems that harm patients. Large-scale projects focused on one kind of quality problem simply cannot lead to significantly better, sustained overall progress for a typical hospital or clinic.

In 1984, the Institute of Medicine estimated 98,000 Americans die each year from medical errors. In September of 2013, new research purports that over the last 30 years, medical errors have grown more than 400 percent, to nearly "400,000 patients annually."[27] By the time you're finished reading this page, two people will have had their lives either altered or ended because of medical errors. "Serious harm seems to be 10- to 20-fold more common than lethal harm, and that epidemic of patient harm in hospitals must be taken more serious!"[28] The increase in harm to patients is happening despite numerous nationwide efforts to reduce medication errors. The same is true of many other classes of preventable harm. The reason for this is clear. There are too many different kinds of problems and causes for "vertical" projects to drive major change. And even when successful, results from such focused projects decay quickly. Instead, many repetitions of a simple improvement cycle that creates different work habits is the *only way* HCOs can make consistent, sustainable success in moving toward greater safety and higher patient satisfaction while dramatically reducing costs.

At AnyWhere in America Hospital, nurses like Bethany struggle with the constant and continued interruptions in the flow of patient care. These costly system failures persist because of the way in which nurses are forced to problem-solve. It is exactly the constant need to work around system problems that creates even more difficulty in taking care of patients. Unknowingly, nurses add to the tide of problems they fight against.[29] And because they cannot care for their patients without jumping the system

---

[27] A New, Evidence-based Estimate of Patient Harms Associated with Hospital Care John T. James, PhD
[28] *Ibid.*
[29] Why Hospitals Don't Learn from Failures: Organizational and Psychological Dynamics that Inhibit

hurdles immediately in their path, priority goes to treating the system failure while their patients wait, absent of the care they need.

This allocation of nurses, a crucial and key resource, is highly irrational. Going back to Econ 101, Adam Smith shows us that the proper division of labor increases productive power, yields higher productivity. Putting this in the context of healthcare, the proper division of labor requires that everyone practice "at the top of their licenses." Specifically, a nurse should be engaged in work that makes maximum use of her expert judgment *about patients*--and not about how to "work the system."

On average, a nurse experiences 6.5 process failures every eight hours. Associated costs range broadly and are factor dependent. However, "a calculated average cost per failure equals $117."[30] If you take that cost and extrapolate the expense across a typical patient census of just 70 percent, nationwide, US Hospitals waste more than $45 billion each year to lost productivity. To make matters worse, this waste of nurses as a precious resource leads to sub-par customer service. No other customer-service industry in America would accept the often poor experience reported by our customers--patients and their loved ones. And even now, as good things are happening in healthcare, nurses are still being burnt out.

Clearly, leaders cannot know enough about the nitty-gritty specifics to make decisions the way that they would like to, but they can go observe to learn how they can best fit into the overall picture of treating nurses as customers. Below we present the

System Change. Anita L. Tucker & Amy C. Edmondson: California Management Review, Vol. 4 No. 7. Winter 2001

[30] The impact of operational failures on hospital nurses and their patients. Anita L. Tucker. Journal of Operations Management 22 (2004) 151–169

beginnings of an alternative approach to leading--the context being that leaders' perceived view of just how the work functions is all too often in conflict with their dashboards. The most important point is that managers have to start solving problems by seeking to understand. And it's from this new understanding that creative advances in delivering optimal value emerge.

The Connection between Nurses and Services

The process diagram below is the simplest depiction of the customer-supplier relationship. It starts with the patient, the nurse, and then support services, until, finally, it returns to the patient. This simple diagram is a guide, as work is made clear, so too are these relationships. Defining the customer-supplier relationship starts here.

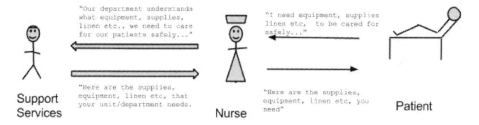

by Wendi Andersohn

Seeing is Believing

To begin understanding differently, leaders and managers should go observe work as it actually happens. There are two elements of preparation for you to begin to do this. First, find a location and a person to observe. This is best done by talking to a local manager to get both their approval and to allow them to select a staff person who will most readily handle "management" watching and asking questions. Second, you will need to prepare yourself. Documentation of your observations is key to recalling the good information you will learn, and will be instrumental to you later when managers work with nurses--and other frontline staff--to eliminate the problems causing process failures and delayed patient care. In this exercise, you'll be observing the activities of one nurse for an hour and documenting minute-by-minute.

How to layout your observation tool

The layout of your document is below starting from the left side of a standard sheet of lined paper.

1. The left-hand column lists the 60 minutes on the clock :00 through :59.

2. The next column records where they worked (i.e., patient room, med station) during that minute.

3. The third column is where you record what task(s) they were working on during that minutes time.

4. The following column, "Who", is a list of the people they interacted with

5. The Last column is for you to tally how many topics, were covered in their interactions with other people.

Your observations should be directed at understanding the actual facts on the ground, while showing respect for the work of nurses and others who take care of patients. By allowing yourself to see the world from a nurse's perspective during a series of these observations, you'll not only be enlightened, but you'll start positive job relationships that can continually be built upon.

However, this kind of observation will also require you to hold back. You aren't going out to see what's wrong and fix it, and you're not there to criticize. You can (and should) ask lots of questions about how they know where to find things; what they will do next; where they got information from; or what they do when they find themselves in a bind, and so on. You should avoid asking "why" questions--since these tend to put people in a defensive position. Also, you should not correct or intervene during your observation. The only exception to this is if you see that some kind of harm will come to someone. Again, you are there to learn. Learning about safety and/or policy violations that are actually happening are a gift to you as a leader. Jump in to correct or intervene, and you will crush that opportunity. Finally, the observee is in charge of the observation. If the observee wants a bit of space or to end the observation, you defer to them. You are there as learner. They are teaching you about how work really happens, and they control the teaching environment.

In the thousands of hour-long observations we and our colleagues have performed that track the movement, interactions, and topics of discussion among nurses the following patterns are shockingly consistent.[31]

- Approximately 12 minutes of each hour is spent documenting, often called "indirect patient care," though much of this consists of feeding information into a

[31] Put another way, the median is the mode.

45

computer system that works well for auditing/report generation and billing, but not for clinical support.[32]

- Roughly 32 minutes is spent "treating the system"--finding missing supplies, missing patients, missing ancillary service, receiving the wrong person, the wrong information, etc.
- The fraction that remains (16 minutes) is what a nurse has available to interact face-to-face with her five or often more patients.

One of us (Baird), after having a conversation with a highly motivated nurse manager, learned there were countless times where, as a floor nurse, she had run out of supplies, and many times she had hustled off to other departments to get what she needed. The manager recalled one particular shift when she ran out of supplies--only this time, so too did several other nurses in her department. The group put together a list of supplies they needed for their patients, then selected one of them to go retrieve them.

With the list in hand, the manager recalls, she headed down to Materials Management. Walking in, she saw that no one was available to assist her, so she decided to get what she needed anyway. As she was searching around for the supplies she needed, she heard a sound coming from another aisle directly behind her. Curious, the nurse walked to the end of the aisle to investigate, only to discover two other nurses from other departments looking through shelves of supplies trying to find what they

---

[32] The approximately 12 minutes per hour spent in documentation are often called "indirect patient care"-- though much of this really feeds state and local legal requirements and feeds information into a computer system that well designed for auditing/report generation and billing.

46

needed.

Nurses, frustrated by the sheer number of problems they face, can and do create elaborate means and methods to protect themselves and their patients from the constant issues caused by current system failures. Some of these techniques include hoarding supplies, hiding equipment, and taking supplies and equipment from other departments. Resorting to this problem-solving method makes patient care exceedingly inefficient and unconscionably expensive.

Much worse, the services essential to smoothing a nurse's work making it easy for the nurse to do the right thing for her patient the first time, every time are under constant pressure to do more with less. In fact, we've seen services like Central Medical Equipment, Materials Management, Linen Department, Central Processing, and Environmental Services so overwhelmed by their own internal process failures that nurses are essentially used as back-up staff--cleaning equipment, shuttling materials, or transporting and waiting with patients in another department.[33] The essence of system functionality is operational, not financial. How local systems operate together, inside the larger system, is key to understanding early, and reaching quickly, the goal of lowering operational costs and increasing the quality of patient care in the United States.

Setting a Focus

It might seem from the preceding section that focus cannot work. There are too many kinds of problems for it to be effective. However, choosing a focus is not a way to

---

[33] Notice that this is a colossal misallocation of resources. The focus on unit efficiency—as opposed to overall system operational smoothness--results in vastly higher labor costs. Not only that, it takes skilled clinicians away from their other patients.

eliminate all other efforts in the organization--there will always be many important things that require effort and attention. Rather, focus is a way to use an existing strategic imperative as the opportunity to create capabilities throughout the organization. Focusing is taking something that already matters to organizational success and devoting a little extra time and effort to it for a defined period of time--typically a year. Leaders must commit themselves and their managers to devote a little more time and effort to creating a learning environment and to start transforming care and the working conditions of all healthcare workers--especially nurses. Once leaders have examined the work from the perspective of a nurse, as it really happens, managers will have a deeper understanding of their own job, role, and new responsibilities.

With a focus set, leaders guide managers through a process of setting intermediate goals that will further the organizational focus. These goals should be within a manager's span of control and represent a "good bet" that it will positively impact the focal strategic imperative set by leadership. For example, say the senior team examines its HCAHPS scores from the past and decides the organization needs to improve its scores on pain management. They then narrow down those scores and identifies a very specific lagging goal: to go from 60 percent "My pain was well managed" to 85 percent--about the point where the organization will receive extra money for exceptional performance. The senior team shares this specific goal and leads managers to set targeted goals within their own span of control. For example, Pharmacy would commit to reducing stock-outs of pain meds from three per month to one per month; a nursing unit would commit to every-two-hour checks on patients' pain status, and so on. Each frontline manager would establish a similar simple and immediately measurable goal. If the goal is out of their span of control or requires a lot of data gathering, senior leaders must redirect them. The key for senior leaders is to get the ball rolling on problem solving toward these smaller goals.

To be clear, senior leaders and executives should not get involved in frontline problem solving, unless their authority is needed. A proper division of labor is essential to sustainable success. Senior leaders should do four important things: set the focal goal for the organization; hold the goals steady, even when their folks exceed expectations; create and maintain focus as described above, without letting their managers off the hook for the many other jobs they're responsible for; and finally, "clear the path" of political landmines and red tape.

One other guideline is that frontline managers should be sure to start their efforts by focusing on the overburden on nurses. To do this, require nurses to communicate to their managers when something related to the focus is not working properly. For example, if an IV pump is stocked-out--which affects patients' pain and subsequent pain scores--a nurse reports this immediately to her manager. The manager will then quickly help to resolve the immediate problem and then use the method we describe below to clarify the cause(s) of the missing pump, ultimately leading to tested and agreed-upon measures that eliminate the cause(s).

With more time on their units, frontline managers not only start to create a smoother working system for nurses and the patients they care for, they also start to change the way they approach their work. Most managers tend to place problems

49

squarely on the shoulders of a person or department--"they just forgot" or "they didn't bring us the right thing." But this is counterproductive, since resolving a problem by lobbing it over the wall to another part of the organization does nothing to get at the real cause of the problem. Alternatively, we've seen managers rush to a fix without really understanding the problem or its cause--meaning that the "fix" doesn't really work or requires constant reminders or complaint emails. In this new focused framework, managers will take more time and care investigating the cause of the specific problem, focused on the patient. They would start with something like, "Today the patient in Room 464 had to wait for IV medications." Although seemingly counterintuitive, a manager focusing on a specific problem and approaching the problem scientifically--the subject of the next chapter--can make much more progress much more quickly on the systemic causes of important and persistent problems.

Chapter 5

Healthcare and the Scientific Method

With a clearly articulated and steadily held focus, senior leaders can teach the organization to approach their own work processes scientifically. In many ways, healthcare is very good at accepting science in the form of clinical guidelines and codified best practices. But the practice of science in work can and should be done at every level of the organization.

As mentioned in Chapter 4, a focus enables everyone in the organization to see more clearly organizational and system barriers or problems--what scientists call "anomalies." In fact, all good science proceeds by attention to anomalies. Science treats anomalies--what is unexplained or contrary to prediction--as an opportunity to create a deeper understanding of the world. Perhaps the most famous example is the Michelson-Morley experiment--sometimes called the most important failed experiment in history. In 1887 Albert Michelson and Edward Morley sought to detect relative motion through "aether," long thought to be the unseen presence explaining the fact that light always moves at a constant speed. In experimenting to test the theory of aether, they unearthed an anomaly: there was no evidence to support the theory. More sophisticated research performed later confirmed this conclusion. The anomaly, rather than being the death-knell of science, set the stage for what is often called the "Second Scientific Revolution." Without the Michelson-Morley experiments there would have been no Einstein--who most certainly changed our understanding of the universe in broad and deep ways.

The Scientific Method and Work

Science gets its start at the base of the pyramid (see diagram below). At first, all we can do is observe the stuff out there in the world. But soon we begin to see patterns, and we create categories. For instance we see many creatures with beaks, feathers, and two legs. Furthermore, we observe that animals with these features can fly. The classification, through observation, leads us to predict that anything with those

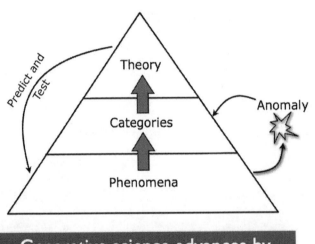

The Scientific Method

Generative science advances by attention to "anomalies."

Source: Christensen & Sundahl,
"A Theory of Theory Building"

characteristics can fly. We have a theory.

The terms "theory" or "theoretical" are often used pejoratively. However, a theory

52

is just a statement of what causes what and why. In this case, we'd say that the physical characteristics of birds enable them to fly. (This is, of course, a rudimentary theory, but a theory nonetheless.) So, moving down the left side of the pyramid in the diagram, we test our theory about birds. As long as we apply the test to each thing that has beaks and feathers and wings and they fly, we continue to shore up the theory. But imagine that one day we go to the South Pole. To our surprise, we find creatures that, although fitting our "able to fly" category, cannot. We must either redefine the category to include them, or place them in another category altogether.

In healthcare, work practices are our theories--they tell us what causes the outcomes we seek. When one of us (Sundahl) first started working in healthcare, he spent time observing housekeepers. What he found was a high degree of variability in work practices. This may not seem important, but take one simple case: how many squirts of cleaner are the right number to clean a sink? It sounds trivial, but Sundahl found that housekeepers squirted a sink anywhere from three to twelve times. If three is the right amount, the hospital was potentially spending four times more than necessary on cleaning solution. In a medium-sized hospital, cutting chemical costs by 75% would be a substantial ongoing savings. Not only that, but the reduction in chemical use would be better for workers and patients. On the other hand, if twelve squirts of solution aren't enough to clean a sink, then no room was ever completely and properly cleaned. We don't mean to indict this organization and its housekeepers. Rather, we wish to point out that because Housekeeping had not yet designed their work as a "theory" to be studied scientifically, this hospital was guaranteed to be doing something harmful, either

53

financially or physically.

Using the Scientific Method to Improve

We and our colleagues have used the scientific method to make progress toward organizational goals. In order to make the scientific method more immediately applicable, we started with an amalgam of best practices and improved them, through much rigorous testing, to arrive at four simple steps. Many people will recognize a similarity to PDSA/PDCA, but our method is based on the scientific method and is more actionable than these very important and influential methodologies.[34] Indeed, it relies on many quick repetitions of the cycle, rather than just one or two.

In the technique we practice and teach, all work is treated as a theory. Each process tests a hypothesis of how to achieve a desired outcome. In the above example of housekeepers, we see that the theory for cleaning a room was not sufficiently clear, and that some actions, in this case applying cleaning chemicals, were not clearly connected to the desired outcome of a clean room.

When each work process is considered as a theory, workers can easily identify "anomalies"--actions or outcomes that do not conform to the work-as-theory. Once an anomaly is identified, there are four steps for rigorously making an improvement.

1. Understand the current condition of the anomaly encountered.

2. Identify the root cause(s) that led to the anomaly.

3. Describe a target condition that will eliminate the specific problem

---

[34] We have also seen recently that "scientific" has become synonymous with the use of sophisticated tools of data analysis. It's important to keep in mind that while skill with data can be useful, it is not a substitute for use of the basics of the scientific method.

and underlying cause.

4. Design and test countermeasures that workers can easily follow.

Turning to another example, if a nurse finds the supply room she is working in is stocked-out of pre-filled syringes, this would be the "anomaly." After quickly helping the nurse obtain the syringe, a manager can start to understand what happened that led to there being no pre-filled syringes available. As she gains understanding, she begins to probe the cause of this breakdown. In practice, we have found that as a leader starts to understand the root cause, they will often need to return to fully understand more about the current condition. Once the current condition and root cause are understood, the manager and her team move to describe a target condition, in which the problem and cause will not recur. Finally, the manager and her team will describe all of the steps required to change the current work practice into the better system, all the while testing their hypotheses about the problem and its causes.

The vast majority of a manager's time should be spent on understanding the anomaly and its causes. Our rule of thumb, which has yielded a great deal of success, is that the first two steps should take 80 percent of the total time devoted to improvement. One of the most significant advantages of this approach, as previously discussed, is that it eliminates problems of "buy in." As commonly structured now, a manager sees a problem and figures out how she wants to change things. Then she has to do the tough job of explaining those changes to many people to get buy in for her decisions--often having to remind people to "follow the process." We have found that if a manager acquires an understanding first and continually validates that understanding with her staff, gaining agreement and compliance on specific countermeasures becomes trivial.

A second counterintuitive task that eliminates disagreements is to focus on the specific issue. Rather than trying to solve the overall problem of the missing pre-filled syringes, which undoubtedly has many different causes, understanding the specific problem and identifying its causes leads to greater agreement on and durability of improvements. The scientific methodology we use and teach focuses on eliminating the causes of problems by looking deeply at a particular case. Consequently, some problems that seem similar must be treated differently, and some issues that appear unrelated will be improved because they arise from the same cause(s).

One final note about the scientific approach: Senior leaders should manage the process and not other people's conclusions or decisions. If a leader tries to second-guess a manager, the manager will be reluctant to dig as deeply as necessary to make an improvement. Furthermore, a senior leader will always--or *should* always--know less than a frontline manager or supervisor about the workings of a specific department or unit. Encouraging managers to take charge in the improvement process by assessing whether they have followed the scientific process with their staff clarifies a manager's value and adds accountability for all involved.

A Real-life Example

In a mid-sized hospital, both of us were involved in helping an organization transform. Senior leaders decided to address their deficit of knowledge, rather than of dollars. Instead of mandating arbitrary, system-wide reductions or purchasing yet another canned solution, these leaders looked within--at their current processes and systems. In doing so, they learned a fundamental truth: operations start with their employees. They also discovered that to solve operational issues, *managers must actively get involved.* Observing the current condition of the work of nurses helped them understand its operational effectiveness and functionality.

The smart leaders from this organization developed a clearly defined problem-solving structure--the scientific method--using a commonly available tool to facilitate staff and management communications. As managers began to observe, they were more able to quickly visualize each role and how it fit into the overall department practices, along with the number and types of failures needing to be addressed. They also learned that due to interconnectedness between internal departmental processes and the larger system-wide processes, imbalances negatively affect nurses and the patients they care for.

Not long after setting the process in motion, they observed that open discussion of problems between managers and staff became the norm. Eventually, staff began to lead improvements. They were trained to observe workflow and understand information relays and intera/interdepartmental communications--just as managers had been at the outset. Staff brought their observations and recommendation to their teams and others throughout the hospital, making significant improvements at a pace much faster than conventional problem solving.

To give you an idea of how this looked, consider a case where the director of pharmacy learned that a vendor was changing the way a particular drug was administered, which had the potential to cause serious harm if incorrectly administered. Rather than issuing an email or putting up billboards or holding in-service meetings, the pharmacist and an coach assigned by senior leaders started by observing nurses administering the medication. After a day's observations, they mocked up instructions for using the new formulation in a Word document. They then sought out many nurses over the course of about an hour, and asked them if they understood the directions. Each time they found something that wasn't right, they went back to the computer, revised it, and printed a new version. After a second hour of this, as well as trials on the night shift, the nurses all said they understood the instructions. Next, the pharmacist put the instructions in the hands of nurses and asked if the directions could be followed easily. After a few rounds of tinkering with the Word document, everyone seemed as though they could follow the proper, safe process without any external prompting. To complete the cycle, the pharmacist and his coach observed the nurses each time the new formulation of the drug was ordered and sent to the floor. They discovered they needed a few more tweaks, and within less than two weeks, they had 100 percent compliance with a new standard that impacted the ease of nurses' work and, more importantly, secured the safety of all patients receiving this medication.

During another observation, Materials Management learned it needed to improve its customer service. The process of moving inventory from the warehouse to the location where it would be consumed was so convoluted that many departments reverted to managing their own inventory. These processes together, they discovered, consumed so much time that nursing floors stocked-out of inventory before the materials handler could return to stock the department. Because there were too many undefined steps, the great deal of variation in how the job was performed was negatively affecting the daily continuity of services, as well as patient care. This meant that patients had to wait for their nurses to address the system failures first before getting care themselves.

To address this, Materials Management separated the processes of counting, picking, delivering, and receiving. The operations of each function were then clearly specified so that a materials handler could accurately understand how each step is connected. They developed a schematic for each job function, incorporating the sequence and the timing necessary to perform each task. They then broke down the staffing matrix and created a new work schematics that matched the new process flows. Since failures were appreciated as opportunities to learn, each time they encountered a problem in the new structure, they embraced it. This created an atmosphere that generated energy for change, and drove their employee satisfaction scores to an all-time high.

One of the most challenging aspects of this approach is that it can be difficult for the organization's leaders to understand. During the course of the turnaround that Baird and my team (along with other leaders and coaches from within the hospital) led there, Baird's colleagues and bosses in Materials Management and Supply Chain saw the results and asked him to come talk to the group. In six months, he had turned a $750,000 loss into a $200,000 gain. They wanted to know how. I ran into Baird after he came back. He seemed a bit frustrated, saying "I don't think I got my message across."

When asked how he had achieved these results, Baird started with the first improvement, which saved the hospital $1,200. This was positively underwhelming for the assembled managers and directors. They just kept saying, "But that's such a small gain, where did you recover the $1 million?" Baird dutifully walked them through more improvements, but it didn't make sense to them.

In the end, Baird encountered two problems that my colleagues and I have found in many places. First, managers are not trained or rewarded to teach and lead improvement efforts. Managers typically succeed through splashy results. Baird was only able to achieve what he did because of the extraordinary vision of the leaders at this hospital. Leaders understood that the repeated process of improvement using the scientific method would inculcate important values and practices, as well as returning substantial desired results. Second, the power of the principles you encounter in this book is only realized through repeated, small applications. Baird implemented hundreds of improvements over that six-month period. And, in total, the hospital executed thousands more. The focus enables an organization to move together toward a shared objective; the scientific method quickly churns out small, durable changes that move toward it. The power of the principles and practices is only realized through the joint effect of many cycles of improvement.

Former CEO and Chairman of Toyota Motors, Fujio Cho, once said, "No mere process can turn a poor performer into a star. Rather, you have to address employees' fundamental way of thinking." The constant repetition of the process, yoked to the focus of the organization, changes not just the way people work, but the way they think. The power of the focus and the method is that they create a coherent system that forms a foundation for continued operational excellence. As many individuals work in a consistent way for the success of the organization, the million little things that get in the way of nurses' work start to disappear, and nurses can spend their considerable energy and intelligence on their patients.

Chapter 6

The Final Connection: A Renewed AWH

A year later, Bethany makes her way to a patient's room after having completed nurse changeover. Knocking first, she opens the door and politely says, "Hello, I'm Bethany, your nurse this evening. How are you feeling?" She logs on to a computer located right next to Darlene, her patient. "Let's see where we are at this evening" "Hmmm. It looks like the doctor ordered IV fluid for you, and an increase to your pain meds. So I'll order in IV fluids, check your vitals, then fetch your medication. How does that sound?"

"Sounds good," Darlene replies, "but I'm a bit hungry, too. Is it okay for me to eat something? It's been hours since I've eaten."

"Would you like me to order something?" Bethany asks.

"Yes, anything is better than nothing," Darlene says, chuckling.

There is a knock on the door and a quiet voice whispers, "Good evening, Central Medical Equipment." The door widens and a woman carrying IV fluid, tubing, a pump and gloves enters. Bethany indicates where to place the items.

After a quick glance, Bethany says, "Everything seems in good working order." Turning to her patient, she says, "Are you ready for your IV?" Within minutes, the IV line is in. Everything is working as expected. "I'll be back, I need to go and retrieve your medication," Bethany explains to Darlene. Suddenly, there is another knock at the door. "Hello, Nutritional Services," the man says as he enters the room.

"Hi, Paul." Bethany says in passing. As Paul enters the room, he waves. Bethany leaves, reiterating to Darlene, "I'll be right back with your meds."

Paul grabs a bedside table, pulling it closer to Darlene, where it will be useful. "I have your soup, crackers, and water," he says, placing them on the table. "If you need anything, use the nurse call button, okay?" Paul tells the patient before leaving.

Bethany knocks quickly before entering. "I have your medication," she says making her way to Darlene's bedside and handing the medication to her.

Before Bethany can say another word, the patient blurts out loudly, "Is this going to cost me more when I get my bill?!" Nervously, she looks to her nurse for a response.

Bethany looks up, smiling, and tells the patient, "You know what? I've been asked that very question many, many times before."

Darlene is confused, but consoled by the fact she isn't the only one asking. Then she explains that she was hospitalized just a year ago at this very same hospital, and the service was deplorable. It took over an hour to get an IV, and she couldn't recall how long it took to get her meds. And for the food, she went on to say, she missed some meals altogether because she was sent for tests during meal times. "How can this very same hospital turn around so drastically and not cost me more?"

"Our leadership changed," Bethany replies. "Oh, I don't mean that literally," she explains. "Our manager came out of her office one day, and she never went back in. And that, made a world of difference. Sure, she goes back to her office every now and then. But today you'll find she's often on the floor, helping nurses like me, help patients, like you." Bethany straightens the covers at the foot of the bed and readjusts the table so Darlene can reach it more easily. "And it wasn't just my manager it was every manager. They just decided to focus on fixing the many small problems nurses faced, one at a time. And then they discovered the byproduct of that focus not only decreased our operational costs, but drastically increased patient satisfaction." Bethany's tone becomes thoughtful. "Treating us like customers of internal services allowed nurses more time to provide better care for less cost, creating value our patients can see and feel. Oh, yeah. And lastly, our own nursing engagement scores, which measure nurses' satisfaction in the workplace, soared! Without this new approach, honestly, I don't know if I would still be working here."

Epilogue

In a hospital located somewhere in America, a young woman, a mother of three children, steps out into a hallway as the elevator door closes behind her. She looks left then right before walking down to the end of the hall to visit her husband. Opening the door, she sees him lying on his side, his back facing her, blood-soaked sheet covering him. Quickly she moves closer, pulling back the sheet and exposing a very large incision that is leaking blood from where a tube had been. Making her way around the other side, she sees his face is agonizingly pale, his eyes closed, his body shaking uncontrollably. *Something has seriously gone wrong she thinks to herself,* trying not to panic as she darts out the door, down the hall to the nursing station, to get help.

"My husband needs help!" she keeps saying. "Something's really wrong with him!" she tells the nurse, who asks her to hold on a moment. The woman looks down at the floor for a moment, thinking he could be in serious trouble. Upset, she looks up again. There, suddenly out of nowhere, a friendly face walks around the corner. It is another nurse--a friend who just happened to be on her way to visit. The woman rushes over quickly, telling her friend the nurse something has gone terribly wrong with her husband. Surprised, the nurse moves quickly with her friend back to the patient's room.

She immediately begins assessing his condition, calling the patient's name over and over with little to no response. The nurse walks around the other side of the bed only to find the pain pump he's attached to is broken. Determined, this nurse sets out to get this patient the care he needs desperately.

It is a haunting memory--one my family and I will ever forget, because I was the patient. A lucky patient at that. But nurses there were not seen as customers of internal services yet. And no consistent focus or methodology grounded practice there. So my family's experience was a regrettably predictable result. If it hadn't been me, it would've been someone else. From that day, I have wished my nurse had the kind of support Bethany came to have. And from my first days as a worker in healthcare, I have seen the awesome responsibility and daily difficulties of nurses. This book, and my work, is for them and for all of us who depend on them.

Chapter 1

Background NO 2779 March 22, 2013

[2] High Food Wastage and Low Nutritional Intakes in Hospital Patients; A. D. Barton, C. L. Beigg, I. A. Macdonald, S. P. Allison: (Clinical Nutrition 2000, 19(6): 445-449) Harcourt Publisher Ltd.

[3] High Food Wastage and Low Nutritional Intakes in Hospital Patients; A. D. Barton, C. L. Beigg, I. A. Macdonald, S. P. Allison: (Clinical Nutrition 2000, 19(6): 445-449) Harcourt Publisher Ltd.

[4] While this may seem implausible to many, both of us have worked for organizations that ran into this very problem. Sundahl worked for a client who touted the cost savings of this system, saying that he had been able reduce materials handlers. As the system failed because "the nurses just won't press the $%*! button," this very smart executive had an a-ha moment. He solved the problem by *hiring people to monitor and manage the machines,* adding back more FTEs than he had cut the previous year by implementing the automated system. If an executive this smart could miss this irony, Sundahl figured anyone could.

[5] For the purposes of this book we are utilizing the nurse (as customer) as they are the recipient of nearly every clinical and non-clinical services or request, which they then provide either directly or indirectly to a patient or physician.

Chapter 2

[6] The Effect of Hospital Nurse Staffing on Patient Health Outcomes: Evidence from California's Minimum Staffing Regulation: Andrew Cook, Martin Gaynor, Melvin Stephens, Jr., and Lowell Taylor NBER Working Paper No. 16077 June 2010 JEL No. I10,I18,J08

[7] *Ibid.*

[8] Nurse Burnout and Patient Satisfaction: Doris C. Vahey, PhD, RN, Linda H. Aiken, PhD, Rn, dougla s M. Sloane, PhD, Sean P.l Clarke, PhD, RN and Defino Vargas, PhD

[9] Hospital Nurse Staffing and Patient Mortality, Nurse Burnout and Job Dissatisfaction; Linda J. Aiken PhD, RN, Sean P. Clarke PhD, RN, Douglass M. Sloane PhD, Julie Sochalski, PhD, RN, Jeffery H. Silber, MD, PhD

[10] From *Solving the Nursing Shortage*, "Listening to Nurses: Dissatisfaction and Burnout on the Job." http://www.afscme.org/news/publications/health-care/solving-the-nursing-shortage/listening-to-nurses-dissatisfaction-and-burnout-on-the-job

[11] Journal of the American Medical Association, June 14, 2000,283 (22): 2948-2954. as cited by Joint Commission on Accreditation of Healthcare Organizations

[12] 5 Buerhaus, Peter, Staiger, Douglas,Auerbach, David,"Implications of an aging RN workforce,"

Journal of the American Medical Association, June 14, 2000,283 (22): 2948-2954.

[13] Aiken LH, Clarke SP, Sloane Dm, Sochalski J, Silber J. Hospital nurse staffing and patient mortality, nurse burnout, and job dissatisfaction. JAMA 2002 Cot 23;288(16); 1987-93

[14] Anderson S. Deadly consequences: the hidden impacts of America's nursing shortage(monograph on the internet). Arlington, VA: National Foundation for American Policy; 2007 Sep {cited 2008 Apr 21}

Chapter 3

[15] Why Hospitals Don't Learn from Failures: ORGANIZATIONAL AND PSYCHOLOGICAL DYNAMICS THAT INHIBIT SYSTEM CHANGE Anita L. Tucker & Amy C. Edmondson: CALIFORNIA MANAGEMENT REVIEW VOl. 4S, NO 7 WINTER 2001

[16] JONA Volume 38, Number 5, pp 230-236 Copyright B 2008 Wolters Kluwer Health | Lippincott Williams & Wilkins THE JOURNAL OF NURSING ADMINISTRATION The Cost of Nurse-Sensitive Adverse Events Sharon Holcombe Pappas, PhD, RN, CNAA, BC
[17] Relationships between Service Providers and Their Impact on Customers, Jody Hoffer Gittell, Journal of S ervice Research 2002 4: 299
18 Ibid.
Although we mostly use hospital settings, there are many environments that constitute an HCO. For instance, in a clinic, it may make sense to think of the physician, medical assistants, PAs or someone else as the central "customer" of other services for patients.
Relationships between Service Providers and Their Impact on Customers, Jody Hoffer Gittell, Journal of Service Research 2002 4: 299
[19] Decoding the DNA of the Toyota Production System by Steven Spear and H. Kent Bowen, HARVARD BUSINESS REVIEW September-October 1999
[19] Relationships between Service Providers and Their Impact on Customers, Jody Hoffer Gittell, Journal of Service Research 2002 4: 299
[21] We borrow here the terminology and guidelines for designing work systems used by Steven Spear and Kent Bowen from their article, "Decoding the DNA of the Toyota Production System."
[22] The details of how to design a reliable system such as this will be covered in more detail in subsequent chapters.

[23] See Speier C, Valacich J, Vessey I. "The Influence of Task Interruption on Individual Decision Making: An Information Overload Perspective." Decision Sciences. 1999; 30(2):337–60.

[24] Details on the method for doing this are below in Chapter 5.

Chapter 4

[25] A New, Evidence-based Estimate of Patient Harms Associated with Hospital Care John T. James, PhD
[26] Ibid.
[27] Why Hospitals Don't Learn from Failures: Organizational and Psychological Dynamics that Inhibit System Change. Anita L. Tucker & Amy C. Edmondson: California Management Review, Vol. 4 No. 7. Winter 2001
[28] The impact of operational failures on hospital nurses and their patients. Anita L. Tucker. Journal of Operations Management 22 (2004) 151–169
[29] Put another way, the median is the mode.
[30] The approximately 12 minutes per hour spent in documentation are often called "indirect patient care"--though much of this really feeds state and local legal requirements and feeds information into a computer system that well designed for auditing/report generation and billing.
[31] Notice that this is a colossal misallocation of resources. The focus on unit efficiency—as opposed to overall system operational smoothness--results in vastly higher labor costs. Not only that, it takes skilled clinicians away from their other patients.

Chapter 5
[32] We have also seen recently that "scientific" has become synonymous with the use of sophisticated tools of data analysis. It's important to keep in mind that while skill with data can be useful, it is not a substitute for use of the basics of the scientific method.